First published in Great Britain by Brockhampton Press,
a member of the Hodder Headline Group,
20 Bloomsbury Street, London WC1B 3QA.

This 1999 edition is published by Gramercy Books™, an imprint of
Random House Value Publishing, Inc., 201 East 50th Street, New York, N.Y. 10022.

Gramercy Books™ and colophon are trademarks of
Random House Value Publishing, Inc.

Random House
New York • Toronto • London • Sydney • Auckland
http://www.randomhouse.com/

Created and produced by Flame Tree Publishing,
part of The Foundry Creative Media Company Limited,
Crabtree Hall, Crabtree Lane, Fulham, London SW6 6TY.

Special thanks to
Kate Brown and Kelley Doak for their work on this series.

Printed and bound in U. A. E.

A CIP catalog record for this book is available from the Library of Congress.

ISBN 0-517-16101-X

8 7 6 5 4 3 2 1

Keats
Truth & Imagination

Written and Compiled by
K. E. SULLIVAN

Gramercy Books
New York

Contents

Introduction

JOHN KEATS was a man of intense spirituality, passionate vision and immeasurable imagination. He lived for just twenty-five years, but left a mark on English literature, on the Romantic movement, that was as pure and true as it was unforgettable. He was a creative genius of undoubtable merit, and a supremely likeable character. He is one of the greatest loved and critically acclaimed poets in the history of the English language.

He was born in London, in 1795, the son of a middle-class livery manager and the eldest of five children. His father died when he was eight and his mother remarried two months later, an act she later appeared to have regretted. Keats was largely brought up by grandparents, and sent away to Clarke's School in Middlesex, where he enjoyed a happy and fulfilling education among like-minded boys. Later he would speak of reading Spenser to the sound of nightingales in the school grounds, and he was inspired and made confident by his academic successes. Keats' mother died from tuberculosis, six years after his father, whereupon his guardians removed him from school and apprenticed him to an apothecary.

Keats was a clever and diligent youth. After studying for a time at Guy's Hospital in London, he easily passed his examinations to become a surgeon, although he never practised medicine. Some of his earliest poems, including 'Imitation of Spenser' and 'On Death', were written as he studied, but, with no pretensions to poetry, his work was fresh and unfettered.

His first published poem, 'O Solitude' was printed in the *Examiner* in London in 1816, just before he graduated, and in the years that followed he accepted his vocation as poet,

cutting the ties with all but his most immediate family in order to do so. The decision to take up a career in poetry was a brave and controversial one. He had no history of poetic success, and his aspirations were founded mainly on personal challenge, encouraged by friends who had recognized the value of his work. Keats befriended some of the most influential literary men of his time, including Wordsworth, Shelley and Leigh Hunt, and he maintained a close relationship with his brothers George and Tom, and with Fanny Brawne, who was to become his inspiration, his lover and his obsession.

While Wordsworth lacked discretion, producing reams of poetry which was often indifferent, Keats was an extravagant connoisseur of the English language, able to knit together words with unbridled elegance and grace. His sensitivity, his vivid comprehension of the fundamental elements of people, places and ideas combined to produce intensely moving and evocative poems, an extraordinary juxtaposition of the languorous and the exciting.

His first volume of poetry was inspired by his friendships with Hunt and Shelley, and it was published in 1817 to almost unanimous silence. *Poems* contained thirty of his first poems, set in an awkward and illogical order, running, it appears, from worst to best, a strategy not designed to attract and hold a reader. Keats experienced the same soar of emotion in the presence of nature as most of the Romantic poets, and had numerous obvious influences at this stage; 'Sleep and Poetry' is, for instance, a youthful attempt at Wordsworthian philosophy. But that collection of his fledgling work heralded his great promise; the pure and absolute celebration, comprehension of the senses is evident even in this early work – space, taste, touch, temperature, smell present an experience that is uniquely Keatsian and came to characterize most of this later work.

Keats matured from this first collection at an extraordinary pace. *Endymion* was published in 1818, but because Keats had been associated with Hunt's Cockney School of Poetry, his efforts were dismissed by many, and fiercely attacked by others, including *Blackwood's Magazine*, who called him a 'bantling' and an 'ignorant and unsettled pretender' to culture. But Keats was fundamentally cultured; although he was the least well educated of the Romantic poets, his philosophy of poetry lay in the belief that art was beauty, or, as he says in 'Ode on a Grecian Urn', 'Beauty is Truth, Truth Beauty'. Of all the Romantics, which included by now Shelley, Byron, Wordsworth and Coleridge, among others, he was the poet most concerned with the nature of the imagination, and the long-term importance of poetry, outside of history.

Keats was chastised by many as a political poet, and since the short span of his life fell under the shadow of the Napoleonic Wars, it is not surprising that political commentary underwrites much of what he wrote. But the clear and overwhelming message in his work is not politics, religion, or indeed the state of the human condition in the Regency period. These are the allusions which underpin his work and which provide evidence of his political and moral leanings, but the beauty of his work lies in its sensual implications, in his exquisite vocabulary and grasp of the English language.

In 1819, Keats wrote *The Eve of St Agnes*, 'La Belle Dame sans Merci', most of the odes, 'Lamia', and *The Fall of Hyperion*, works of resounding maturity and scope. Keats believed that the excellence of art lay in its intensity, but that to him could be a kind of sensual intensity, a warm vagueness which suggested rather than explained, an almost subliminal technique which provided so much of his poetic power.

Keats was eclipsed by personal events throughout his life. He fell deeply and obsessively in love with many women; indeed, he was treated for gonorrhoea at one point. The culmination of his intense feelings was his relationship with Fanny Brawne, a married girl of eighteen who moved in next door. Keats was absorbed by her, deeply and inutterably in love. He was tormented by jealousy, and unhappily, as the early stages of their relationship coincided with illness, he began to associate love with pain and death, and through that religion.

Keats had nursed his brother Tom through consumption, from which he eventually died, and he was well aware of the first signs of the disease. Until he was struck down himself, Keats was a figure of robust good health, happy and full of vigour and charm. He fought against illness, became engaged to Fanny, who left her husband, and then threatened to break off their liaison as his condition worsened. He was fired by fear and despair. He wrote to her, 'Shakespeare always sums up matters in the most sovereign manner. Hamlet's heart was full of such Misery as mine when he said to Ophelia "Go to a nunnery, go go!" Indeed I should like to give up the matter at once – I should like to die. I am sickened at the brute world which you are smiling with. I hate men and women more.'

Keats was extremely ill while preparing his final volume of poetry, *Lamia, Isabella, The Eve of St Agnes and Other Poems*, for press. Its publication in July of 1820 was greeted by the suffering poet with little but indifference, although it did receive a warm critical response. Keats was past caring. 'La Belle Dame sans Merci' had been published in Hunt's paper in 1820. It was a poised and marvellous poem, resplendent with literary allusions and echoes, and yet entirely his own. It had bred some interest among the critical establishment, and its immaculate and unique rhythm had inspired a new respect among his contemporaries.

In the summer of that same year, Keats sailed to Italy to convalesce there. He was unaware of the success which had greeted his work at home, and it would still be many years before he would be acclaimed as one of the greatest of the Romantic poets. His youth, his integrity and his absolutely honest good nature prevented him from taking an arrogant stance. His one great worry was that his overwhelming emotion, particularly in love, may preclude his ever becoming a great poet. It is that emotion, perhaps, that gives his poetry the life that sets it apart from all others.

Keats' last poetic utterance was dictated on his deathbed. They were the words which he wished to have inscribed on his tombstone and they read, 'Here lies one whose name was writ on water'.

Author's Note

John Keats wrote poetry which fills the senses, works as fertile with allusion as they are durable and archetypically Romantic. As his work matured, in his tragically short but prolific career, Keats paid increasing attention to the nature of the imagination and the natural world, which became overwhelming themes in his poetry. This selection, chosen from across his published works, includes some of his greatest poems, in whole or extracted, and provides clear evidence of his developing genius.

Chronology

1795   John Keats born, 31 October.

1798   Wordsworth and Coleridge publish *Lyrical Ballads*.

1804   Death of Keats' father; remarriage of his mother. Keats is sent to live with grandparents.

1810   Death of Keats' mother, of tuberculosis.

1811   Keats leaves Enfield School and is apprenticed to Thomas Hammond, a surgeon.

1815   Keats writes sonnet in honour of Leigh Hunt's release from prison. Begins studies at Guy's Hospital.

1816   Keats' first poem published in the *Examiner* on 5 May. Completes education in medicine 25 July, but foresakes medicine for poetry. Writes 'Sleep and Poetry'.

1817   Keats' *Poems* published on 3 March by C. and J. Ollier. Begins *Endymion*.

1818   Writes *Isabella*. *Endymion* published. Receives vitriolic review in *Blackwood's Edinburgh Magazine*. Begins work on *Hyperion*. Tom Keats, Keats' brother whom he has nursed for several years, dies from tuberculosis.

1819   Writes *The Eve of St Agnes* and the spring odes, *Lamia*, 'To Autumn' and others. Begins *The Fall of Hyperion*. Becomes engaged to Fanny Brawne, his great love.

1820   Falls ill in February. 'La Belle Dame sans Merci' published in the *Indicator* (Hunt's paper). Diagnosed with Tuberculosis. *Lamia, Isabella, The Eve of St Agnes and Other Poems*, published in July. Leaves for Italy to convalesce.

1821   Keats dies, 23 February. Buried in the Protestant Cemetery in Rome, 26 February.

To Hope

WHEN BY my solitary hearth I sit,
And hateful thoughts enwrap my soul in gloom;
When no fair dreams before my 'mind's eye' flit,
And the bare heath of life presents no bloom;
Sweet Hope, ethereal balm upon me shed,
And wave thy silver pinions o'er my head.

Whene'er I wander, at the fall of night,
Where woven boughs shut out the moon's bright ray,
Should sad Despondency my musings fright,
And frown, to drive fair Cheerfulness away,
Peep with the moon-beams through the leafy roof,
And keep that fiend Despondence far aloof.

Should Disappointment, parent of Despair,
Strive for her son to seize my careless heart;
When, like a cloud, he sits upon the air,
Preparing on his spell-bound prey to dart:
Chase him away, sweet Hope, with visage bright,
And fright him as the morning frightens night!

Whene'er the fate of those I hold most dear
Tells to my fearful breast a tale of sorrow,
O bright-eyed Hope, my morbid fancy cheer;
Let me awhile thy sweetest comforts borrow:
Thy heaven-born radiance around me shed,
And wave thy silver pinions o'er my head!

Should e'er unhappy love my bosom pain,
From cruel parents, or relentless fair;
O let me think it is not quite in vain
To sigh out sonnets to the midnight air!
Sweet Hope, ethereal balm upon me shed,
And wave thy silver pinions o'er my head!

In the long vista of the years to roll,
Let me not see our country's honour fade:
O let me see our land retain her soul,
Her pride, her freedom; and not freedom's shade.
From thy bright eyes unusual brightness shed –
Beneath thy pinions canopy my head!

Let me not see the patriot's high bequest,
Great Liberty! how great in plain attire!
With the base purple of a court oppressed,
Bowing her head, and ready to expire:
But let me see thee stoop from heaven on wings
That fill the skies with silver glitterings!

And as, in sparkling majesty, a star
Gilds the bright summit of some gloomy cloud;
Brightening the half-veiled face of heaven afar:
So, when dark thoughts my boding spirit shroud,
Sweet Hope, celestial influence round me shed,
Waving thy silver pinions o'er my head.

On the Grasshopper and Cricket

THE POETRY OF earth is never dead:
When all the birds are faint with the hot sun,
And hide in cooling trees, a voice will run
From hedge to hedge about the new-mown mead –
That is the Grasshopper's. He takes the lead
In summer luxury; he has never done
With his delights, for when tired out with fun
He rests at ease beneath some pleasant weed.
The poetry of earth is ceasing never:
On a lone winter evening, when the frost
Has wrought a silence, from the stove there shrills
The Cricket's song, in warmth increasing ever,
And seems to one in drowsiness half lost,
The Grasshopper's among some grassy hills.

'O Solitude! if I must with thee dwell'

O SOLITUDE! if I must with thee dwell,
Let it not be among the jumbled heap
Of murky buildings; climb with me the steep –
Nature's observatory – whence the dell,
Its flowery slopes, its river's crystal swell,
May seem a span; let me thy vigils keep
'Mongst boughs pavilioned, where the deer's swift leap
Startles the wild bee from the foxglove bell.
But though I'll gladly trace these scenes with thee,
Yet the sweet converse of an innocent mind,
Whose words are images of thoughts refined,
Is my soul's pleasure; and it sure must be
Almost the highest bliss of human-kind,
When to thy haunts two kindred spirits flee.

'To one who has been long in city pent'

TO ONE WHO has been long in city pent,
  'Tis very sweet to look into the fair
And open face of heaven – to breathe a prayer
  Full in the smile of the blue firmament.
Who is more happy, when, with heart's content,

Fatigued he sinks into some pleasant lair
Of wavy grass, and reads a debonair
And gentle tale of love and languishment?
Returning home at evening, with an ear
Catching the notes of Philomel – an eye
Watching the sailing cloudlet's bright career,
He mourns that day so soon has glided by:
E'en like the passage of an angel's tear
That falls through the clear ether silently.

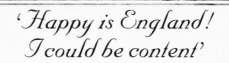

'Happy is England!
I could be content'

HAPPY IS ENGLAND! I could be content
To see no other verdure than its own;
To feel no other breezes than are blown
Through its tall woods with high romances blent;
Yet do I sometimes feel a languishment
For skies Italian, and an inward groan
To sit upon an Alp as on a throne,
And half forget what world or worldling meant.
Happy is England, sweet her artless daughters;
Enough their simple loveliness for me,
Enough their whitest arms in silence clinging:
Yet do I often warmly burn to see
Beauties of deeper glance, and hear their singing,
And float with them about the summer waters.

'How many bards gild the lapses of time!'

HOW MANY bards gild the lapses of time!
A few of them have ever been the food
Of my delighted fancy – I could brood
Over their beauties, earthly, or sublime:
And often, when I sit me down to rhyme,
These will in throngs before my mind intrude:
But no confusion, no disturbance rude
Do they occasion; 'tis a pleasing chime.
So the unnumbered sounds that evening store;
The songs of birds, the whispering of the leaves,
The voice of waters, the great bell that heaves
With solemn sound, and thousand others more,
That distance of recognisance bereaves,
Make pleasing music, and not wild uproar.

On First Looking into Chapman's Homer

MUCH HAVE I travelled in the realms of gold,
And many goodly states and kingdoms seen;
Round many western islands have I been
Which bards in fealty to Apollo hold.
Oft of one wide expanse had I been told
That deep-browed Homer ruled as his demesne;
Yet did I never breathe its pure serene
Till I heard Chapman speak out loud and bold:
Then felt I like some watcher of the skies
When a new planet swims into his ken;
Or like stout Cortez when with eagle eyes
He stared at the Pacific – and all his men
Looked at each other with a wild surmise –
Silent, upon a peak in Darien.

'Keen, fitful gusts are whispering here and there'

KEEN, FITFUL GUSTS are whispering here and there
Among the bushes half leafless, and dry;
The stars look very cold about the sky,
And I have many miles on foot to fare.
Yet feel I little of the cool bleak air,
Or of the dead leaves rustling drearily,
Or of those silver lamps that burn on high,
Or of the distance from home's pleasant lair:
For I am brimful of the friendliness
That in a little cottage I have found;
Of fair-haired Milton's eloquent distress,
And all his love for gentle Lycid drowned;
Of lovely Laura in her light green dress,
And faithful Petrarch gloriously crowned.

Ode on Melancholy

NO, NO, GO NOT to Lethe, neither twist
Wolf's-bane, tight-rooted, for its poisonous wine:
Nor suffer thy pale forehead to be kissed
By nightshade, ruby grape of Proserpine;
Make not your rosary of yew-berries,
Nor let the beetle, nor the death-moth be
Your mournful Psyche, nor the downy owl
A partner in your sorrow's mysteries;
For shade to shade will come too drowsily,
And drown the wakeful anguish of the soul.

But when the melancholy fit shall fall
Sudden from heaven like a weeping cloud,
That fosters the droop-headed flowers all,
And hides the green hill in an April shroud;
Then glut thy sorrow on a morning rose,
Or on the rainbow of the salt sand-wave,
Or on the wealth of globed peonies;
Or if thy mistress some rich anger shows,
Emprison her soft hand, and let her rave,
And feed deep, deep upon her peerless eyes.

She dwells with Beauty – Beauty that must die;
And Joy, whose hand is ever at his lips
Bidding adieu; and aching Pleasure nigh,
Turning to poison while the bee-mouth sips:
Ay, in the very temple of Delight
Veiled Melancholy has her sovran shrine,
Though seen of none save him whose strenuous tongue
Can burst Joy's grape against his palate fine;
His soul shall taste the sadness of her might,
And be among her cloudy trophies hung.

Ode on a Grecian Urn

THOU STILL unravished bride of quietness,
Thou foster-child of silence and slow time,
Sylvan historian, who canst thus express
A flowery tale more sweetly than our rhyme:
What leaf-fringed legend haunts about thy shape
Of deities or mortals, or of both,
In Temple or the dales of Arcady?
What men or gods are these? What maidens loth?
What mad pursuit? What struggle to escape?
What pipes and timbrels? What wild ecstasy?

Heard melodies are sweet, but those unheard
Are sweeter; therefore, ye soft pipes, play on;
Not to the sensual ear, but, more endeared,
Pipe to the spirit ditties of no tone:
Fair youth, beneath the trees, thou canst not leave
Thy song, nor ever can those trees be bare;
Bold Lover, never, never canst thou kiss,
Though winning near the goal – yet, do not grieve:
She cannot fade, though thou hast not thy bliss,
For ever wilt thou love, and she be fair!

Ah, happy, happy boughs! that cannot shed
Your leaves, nor ever bid the Spring adieu;
And, happy melodist, unwearied,
For ever piping songs for ever new;
More happy love! more happy, happy love!
For ever warm and still to be enjoyed,
For ever panting, and for ever young –
All breathing human passion far above,
That leaves a heart high-sorrowful and cloyed,
A burning forehead, and a parching tongue.

Who are these coming to the sacrifice?
To what green altar, O mysterious priest,
Lead'st thou that heifer lowing at the skies,
And all her silken flanks with garlands dressed?
What little town by river or sea shore,
Or mountain-built with peaceful citadel,
Is emptied of this folk, this pious morn?
And, little town, thy streets for evermore
Will silent be; and not a soul to tell
Why thou art desolate, can e'er return.

O Attic shape! Fair attitude! with brede
Of marble men and maidens overwrought,
With forest branches and the trodden weed;
Thou, silent form, dost tease us out of thought
As doth eternity: Cold Pastoral!
When old age shall this generation waste,
Thou shalt remain, in midst of other woe
Than ours, a friend to man, to whom thou say'st,
'Beauty is truth, truth beauty,' – that is all
Ye know on earth, and all ye need to know.'

Ode to a Nightingale

MY HEART ACHES, and a drowsy numbness pains
My sense, as though of hemlock I had drunk,
Or emptied some dull opiate to the drains
One minute past, and Lethe-wards had sunk:
'Tis not through envy of thy happy lot,
But being too happy in thine happiness -
That thou, light-winged Dryad of the trees,
In some melodious plot
Of beechen green, and shadows numberless,
Singest of summer in full-throated ease.

O, for a draught of vintage! that hath been
Cooled a long age in the deep-delved earth,
Tasting of Flora and the country green,
Dance, and Provençal song, and sunburnt mirth!
O for a beaker full of the warm South,
Full of the true, the blushful Hippocrene,
With beaded bubbles winking at the brim,
And purple-stained mouth,
That I might drink, and leave the world unseen,
And with thee fade away into the forest dim –

Fade far away, dissolve, and quite forget
What thou among the leaves hast never known,
The weariness, the fever, and the fret
Here, where men sit and hear each other groan;
Where palsy shakes a few, sad, last grey hairs,
Where youth grows pale, and spectre-thin, and dies;
Where but to think is to be full of sorrow
And leaden-eyed despairs;
Where Beauty cannot keep her lustrous eyes,
Or new Love pine at them beyond to-morrow.

Away! away! for I will fly to thee,
Not charioted by Bacchus and his pards,
But on the viewless wings of Poesy,
Though the dull brain perplexes and retards.
Already with thee! tender is the night,
And haply the Queen-Moon is on her throne,
Clustered around by all her starry Fays;
But here there is no light,
Save what from heaven is with the breezes blown
Through verdurous glooms and winding mossy ways.

I cannot see what flowers are at my feet,
Nor what soft incense hangs upon the boughs,
But, in embalmed darkness, guess each sweet
Wherewith the seasonable month endows
The grass, the thicket, and the fruit-tree wild –
White hawthorn, and the pastoral eglantine;
Fast fading violets covered up in leaves;
And mid-May's eldest child,
The coming musk-rose, full of dewy wine,
The murmurous haunt of flies on summer eves.

Darkling I listen; and, for many a time
I have been half in love with easeful Death,
Called him soft names in many a mused rhyme,
To take into the air my quiet breath;
Now more than ever seems it rich to die,
To cease upon the midnight with no pain,
While thou art pouring forth thy soul abroad
In such an ecstasy!
Still wouldst thou sing, and I have ears in vain –
To thy high requiem become a sod.

Thou wast not born for death, immortal Bird!
No hungry generations tread thee down;
The voice I hear this passing night was heard
In ancient days by emperor and clown:
Perhaps the self-same song that found a path
Through the sad heart of Ruth, when, sick for home,
She stood in tears amid the alien corn;
The same that oft-times hath
Charm'd magic casements, opening on the foam
Of perilous seas, in faery lands forlorn.

Forlorn! the very word is like a bell
To toll me back from thee to my sole self!
Adieu! the fancy cannot cheat so well
As she is fam'd to do, deceiving elf.
Adieu! adieu! thy plaintive anthem fades
Past the near meadows, over the still stream,
Up the hill-side; and now 'tis buried deep
In the next valley-glades:
Was it a vision, or a waking dream?
Fled is that music: – Do I wake or sleep?

To Autumn

SEASON OF MISTS and mellow fruitfulness,
Close bosom-friend of the maturing sun,
Conspiring with him how to load and bless
With fruit the vines that round the thatch-eves run;
To bend with apples the mossed cottage-trees,
And fill all fruit with ripeness to the core;
To swell the gourd, and plump the hazel shells
With a sweet kernel; to set budding more,
And still more, later flowers for the bees,
Until they think warm days will never cease,
For Summer has o'er-brimmed their clammy cells.

Who hath not seen thee oft amid thy store?
Sometimes whoever seeks abroad may find
Thee sitting careless on a granary floor,
Thy hair soft-lifted by the winnowing wind;
Or on a half-reaped furrow sound asleep,
Drowsed with the fume of poppies, while thy hook
Spares the next swath and all its twined flowers;
And sometimes like a gleaner thou dost keep
Steady thy laden head across a brook;
Or by a cider-press, with patient look,
Thou watchest the last oozings hours by hours.

Where are the songs of Spring? Ay, where are they?
Think not of them, thou hast thy music too –
While barred clouds bloom the soft-dying day,
And touch the stubble-plains with rosy hue:
Then in a wailful choir the small gnats mourn
Among the river sallows, borne aloft
Or sinking as the light wind lives or dies;
And full-grown lambs loud bleat from hilly bourn;
Hedge-crickets sing; and now with treble soft
The red-breast whistles from a garden-croft;
And gathering swallows twitter in the skies.

Stanzas

YOU SAY YOU LOVE; but with a voice
Chaster than a nun's, who singeth
The soft Vespers to herself
While the chime-bell ringeth –
O love me truly!

You say you love; but with a smile
Cold as sunrise in September,
As you were Saint Cupid's nun,
And kept his weeks of Ember.
O love me truly!

You say you love; but then your lips
Coral tinted teach no blisses
More than coral in the sea –
They never pout for kisses –
O love me truly!

You say you love; but then your hand
No soft squeeze for squeeze returneth,
It is like a statue's, dead –
While mine for passion burneth –
O love me truly!

O breathe a word or two of fire!
Smile, as if those words should burn me,
Squeeze as lovers should - O kiss
And in thy heart inurn me!
O love me truly!

Fancy

EVER LET the Fancy roam,
Pleasure never is at home:
At a touch sweet Pleasure melteth,
Like to bubbles when rain pelteth.
Then let winged Fancy wander
Through the thought still spread beyond her:
Open wide the mind's cage-door,
She'll dart forth, and cloudward soar.
O sweet Fancy! let her loose —
Summer's joys are spoilt by use,
And the enjoying of the Spring
Fades as does its blossoming;
Autumn's red lipped fruitage too,
Blushing through the mist and dew,
Cloys with tasting. What do then?
Sit thee by the ingle, when
The sere faggot blazes bright,
Spirit of a winter's night;
When the soundless earth is muffled,
And the caked snow is shuffled,
From the ploughboy's heavy shoon;
When the Night doth meet the Noon
In a dark conspiracy
To banish Even from her sky.
Sit thee there, and send abroad,
With a mind self-overawed,
Fancy, high-commissioned — send her!
She has vassals to attend her:
She will bring, in spite of frost,
Beauties that the earth hath lost;
She will bring thee, all together,

All delights of summer weather;
All the buds and bells of May,
From dewy sward or thorny spray;
All the heaped Autumn's wealth,
With a still, mysterious stealth:
She will mix these pleasures up
Like three fit wines in a cup,
And thou shalt quaff it – thou shalt hear
Distant harvest-carols clear;
Rustle of the reaped corn;
Sweet birds antheming the morn:
And, in the same moment – hark!
'Tis the early April lark,
Or the rooks, with busy caw,
Foraging for sticks and straw.
Thou shalt, at one glance, behold
The daisy and the marigold;
White-plumed lilies, and the first
Hedge-grown primrose that hath burst;
Shaded hyacinth, alway
Sapphire queen of the mid-May;
And every leaf, and every flower
Pearled with the self-same shower.
Thou shalt see the field-mouse peep
Meagre from its celled sleep;
And the snake all winter-thin
Cast on sunny bank its skin;
Freckled nest-eggs thou shalt see
Hatching in the hawthorn-tree,
When the hen-bird's wing doth rest
Quiet on her mossy nest;
Then the hurry and alarm
When the bee-hive casts its swarm;
Acorn ripe down-pattering,
While the autumn breezes sing.

O, sweet Fancy! let her loose;
Every thing is spoilt by use:
Where's the cheek that doth not fade,
Too much gazed at? Where's the maid
Whose lip mature is ever new?
Where's the eye, however blue,
Doth not weary? Where's the face
One would meet in every place?
Where's the voice, however soft,
One would hear so very oft?
At a touch sweet Pleasure melteth
Like to bubbles when rain pelteth.
Let, then, winged Fancy find
Thee a mistress to thy mind:
Dulcet-eyed as Ceres' daughter,
Ere the God of Torment taught her
How to frown and how to chide;
With a waist and with a side
White as Hebe's, when her zone
Slipped its golden clasp, and down
Fell her kirtle to her feet,
While she held the goblet sweet,
And Jove grew languid. – Break the mesh
Of the Fancy's silken leash;
Quickly break her prison-string
And such joys as these she'll bring.
Let the winged Fancy roam,
Pleasure never is at home.

Ode

Bards of passion and of Mirth,
Ye have left your souls on earth!
Have ye souls in heaven too,
Double-lived in regions new?
Yes, and those of heaven commune
With the spheres of sun and moon;
With the noise of fountains wondrous,
And the parle of voices thund'rous;
With the whisper of heaven's trees
And one another, in soft ease
Seated on Elysian lawns
Browsed by none but Dian's fawns;
Underneath large blue-bells tented,
Where the daisies are rose-scented,
And the rose herself has got
Perfume which on earth is not;
Where the nightingale doth sing
Not a senseless, tranced thing,
But divine melodious truth;
Philosophic numbers smooth;
Tales and golden histories
Of heaven and its mysteries.

Thus ye live on high, and then
On the earth ye live again;
And the souls ye left behind you
Teach us, here, the way to find you,
Where your other souls are joying,
Never slumbered, never cloying.
Here, your earth-born souls still speak
To mortals, of their little week;
Of their sorrows and delights;
Of their passions and their spites;
Of their glory and their shame;
What doth strengthen and what maim.
Thus ye teach us, every day,
Wisdom, though fled far away.

Bards of passion and of Mirth,
Ye have left your souls on earth!
Ye have souls in heaven too,
Double-lived in regions new!

Ode to Psyche

O GODDESS! hear these tuneless numbers, wrung
By sweet enforcement and remembrance dear,
And pardon that thy secrets should be sung
Even into thine own soft-conched ear:
Surely I dreamt to-day, or did I see
The winged Psyche with awakened eyes?
I wandered in a forest thoughtlessly,
And, on the sudden, fainting with surprise,
Saw two fair creatures, couched side by side
In deepest grass, beneath the whispering roof
Of leaves and trembled blossoms, where there ran
A brooklet, scarce espied:
Mid hushed, cool-rooted flowers, fragrant-eyed,
Blue, silver-white, and budded Tyrian,
They lay calm-breathing on the bedded grass;
Their arms embraced, and their pinions too;
Their lips touched not, but had not bade adieu,
As if disjoined by soft-handed slumber,
And ready still past kisses to outnumber
At tender eye-dawn of aurorean love:
The winged boy I knew;
But who wast thou, O happy, happy dove?
His Psyche true!

O latest born and loveliest vision far
Of all Olympus' faded hierarchy!
Fairer than Phoebe's sapphire-regioned star,
Or Vesper, amorous glow-worm of the sky;
Fairer than these, though temple thou hast none,
Nor altar heaped with flowers;
Nor virgin-choir to make delicious moan
Upon the midnight hours;
No voice, no lute, no pipe, no incense sweet
From chain-swung censer teeming;
No shrine, no grove, no oracle, no heat
Of pale-mouthed prophet dreaming.

O brightest! though too late for antique vows,
Too, too late for the fond believing lyre,
When holy were the haunted forest boughs,
Holy the air, the water, and the fire;
Yet even in these days so far retired
From happy pieties, thy lucent fans,
Fluttering among the faint Olympians,
I see, and sing, by my own eyes inspired.
So let me be thy choir, and make a moan
Upon the midnight hours;
Thy voice, thy lute, thy pipe, thy incense sweet
From swinged censer teeming –
Thy shrine, thy grove, thy oracle, thy heat
Of pale-mouthed prophet dreaming.

Yes, I will be thy priest, and build a fane
In some untrodden region of my mind,
Where branched thoughts, new grown with pleasant pain,
Instead of pines shall murmur in the wind:
Far, far around shall those dark-clustered trees
Fledge the wild-ridged mountains steep by steep;
And there by zephyrs, streams, and birds, and bees,
The moss-lain Dryads shall be lulled to sleep;
And in the midst of this wide quietness
A rosy sanctuary will I dress
With the wreathed trellis of a working brain,
With buds, and bells, and stars without a name,
With all the gardener Fancy e'er could feign,
Who breeding flowers, will never breed the same:
And there shall be for thee all soft delight
That shadowy thought can win,
A bright torch, and a casement ope at night,
To let the warm Love in!

Isabella, or, The Pot of Basil

I

FAIR ISABEL, poor simple Isabel!
Lorenzo, a young palmer in Love's eye!
They could not in the self-same mansion dwell
Without some stir of heart, some malady;
They could not sit at meals but feel how well
It soothed each to be the other by;
They could not, sure, beneath the same roof sleep
But to each other dream, and nightly weep.

II

With every morn their love grew tenderer,
With every eve deeper and tenderer still;
He might not in house, field, or garden stir,
But her full shape would all his seeing fill;
And his continual voice was pleasanter
To her than noise of trees or hidden rill;
Her lute-string gave an echo of his name,
She spoilt her half-done broidery with the same.

III

He knew whose gentle hand was at the latch
Before the door had given her to his eyes;
And from her chamber-window he would catch
Her beauty farther than the falcon spies;
And constant as her vespers would he watch,
Because her face was turned to the same skies;
And with sick longing all the night outwear,
To hear her morning-step upon the stair.

IV

A whole long month of May in this sad plight
Made their cheeks paler by the break of June:
　　'To-morrow will I bow to my delight,
　　To-morrow will I ask my lady's boon.'
　　'O may I never see another night,
　　Lorenzo, if thy lips breathe not love's tune.'
　　So spake they to their pillows; but, alas,
　　Honeyless days and days did he let pass –

V

　　Until sweet Isabella's untouched cheek
　　Fell sick within the rose's just domain,
Fell thin as a young mother's, who doth seek
　　By every lull to cool her infant's pain:
　　'How ill she is,' said he, 'I may not speak,
　　And yet I will, and tell my love all plain:
If looks speak love-laws, I will drink her tears,
　　And at the least 'twill startle off her cares.'

VI

　　So said he one fair morning, and all day
　　His heart beat awfully against his side;
　　And to his heart he inwardly did pray
For power to speak; but still the ruddy tide
Stifled his voice, and pulsed resolve away –
　　Fevered his high conceit of such a bride,
Yet brought him to the meekness of a child:
　　Alas! when passion is both meek and wild!

VII

So once more he had waked and anguished
A dreary night of love and misery,
If Isabel's quick eye had not been wed
To every symbol on his forehead high.
She saw it waxing very pale and dead,
And straight all flushed; so, lisped tenderly,
'Lorenzo!' – here she ceased her timid quest,
But in her tone and look he read the rest.

VIII

'O Isabella, I can half-perceive
That I may speak my grief into thine ear.
If thou didst ever anything believe,
Believe how I love thee, believe how near
My soul is to its doom: I would not grieve
Thy hand by unwelcome pressing, would not fear
Thine eyes by gazing; but I cannot live
Another night, and not my passion shrive.

IX

Love! thou art leading me from wintry cold,
Lady! thou leadest me to summer clime,
And I must taste the blossoms that unfold
In its ripe warmth this gracious morning time.'
So said, his erewhile timid lips grew bold,
And poesied with hers in dewy rhyme:
Great bliss was with them, and great happiness
Grew, like a lusty flower, in June's caress.

X

Parting they seemed to tread upon the air,
Twin roses by the zephyr blown apart
Only to meet again more close, and share
The inward fragrance of each other's heart.
She, to her chamber gone, a ditty fair
Sang, of delicious love and honeyed dart;
He with light steps went up a western hill,
And bade the sun farewell, and joyed his fill.

XI

All close they met again, before the dusk
Had taken from the stars its pleasant veil,
All close they met, all eves, before the dusk
Had taken from the stars its pleasant veil,
Close in a bower of hyacinth and musk,
Unknown of any, free from whispering tale.
Ah! better had it been for ever so,
Than idle ears should pleasure in their woe.

XII

Were they unhappy then? – It cannot be –
Too many tears for lovers have been shed,
Too many sighs give we to them in fee,
Too much of pity after they are dead,
Too many doleful stories do we see,
Whose matter in bright gold were best be read;
Except in such a page where Theseus' spouse
Over the pathless waves towards him bows.

XIII

But, for the general award of love,
The little sweet doth kill much bitterness;
Though Dido silent is in under-grove,
And Isabella's was a great distress,
Though young Lorenzo in warm Indian clove
Was not embalmed, this truth is not the less -
Even bees, the little almsmen of spring-bowers,
Know there is richest juice in poison-flowers.

XIV

With her two brothers this fair lady dwelt,
Enriched from ancestral merchandise,
And for them many a weary hand did swelt
In torched mines and noisy factories,
And many once proud-quivered loins did melt
In blood from stinging whip – with hollow eyes
Many all day in dazzling river stood,
To take the rich-ored driftings of the flood.

XV

For them the Ceylon diver held his breath,
And went all naked to the hungry shark;
For them his ears gushed blood; for them in death
The seal on the cold ice with piteous bark
Lay full of darts; for them alone did seethe
A thousand men in troubles wide and dark:
Half-ignorant, they turned an easy wheel,
That set sharp racks at work to pinch and peel.

XVI

Why were they proud? Because their marble founts
   Gushed with more pride than do a wretch's tears? —
Why were they proud? Because fair orange-mounts
   Were of more soft ascent than lazar stairs? —
Why were they proud? Because red-lined accounts
   Were richer than the songs of Grecian years? —
   Why were they proud? again we ask aloud,
   Why in the name of Glory were they proud?

XVII

   Yet were these Florentines as self-retired
   In hungry pride and gainful cowardice,
   As two close Hebrews in that land inspired,
   Paled in and vineyarded from beggar-spies —
   The hawks of ship-mast forests — the untired
   And panniered mules for ducats and old lies —
   Quick cat's-paws on the generous stray-away —
   Great wits in Spanish, Tuscan, and Malay.

XVIII

   How was it these same ledger-men could spy
   Fair Isabella in her downy nest?
   How could they find out in Lorenzo's eye
   A straying from his toil? Hot Egypt's pest
   Into their vision covetous and sly!
How could these money-bags see east and west? —
   Yet so they did — and every dealer fair
   Must see behind, as doth the hunted hare.

XIX

O eloquent and famed Boccaccio!
Of thee we now should ask forgiving boon,
And of thy spicy myrtles as they blow,
And of thy roses amorous of the moon,
And of thy lilies, that do paler grow
Now they can no more hear thy gittern's tune.
For venturing syllables that ill beseem
The quiet glooms of such a piteous theme.

XX

Grant thou a pardon here, and then the tale
Shall move on soberly, as it is meet;
There is no other crime, no mad assail
To make old prose in modern rhyme more sweet:
But it is done – succeed the verse or fail –
To honour thee, and thy gone spirit greet,
To stead thee as a verse in English tongue,
An echo of thee in the north wind sung.

XXI

These brethren having found by many signs
What love Lorenzo for their sister had,
And how she loved him too, each unconfines
His bitter thoughts to other, well nigh mad
That he, the servant of their trade designs,
Should in their sister's love be blithe and glad,
When 'twas their plan to coax her by degrees
To some high noble and his olive-trees.

XXII

And many a jealous conference had they,
And many times they bit their lips alone,
Before they fixed upon a surest way
To make the youngster for his crime atone;
And at the last, these men of cruel clay
Cut Mercy with a sharp knife to the bone,
For they resolved in some forest dim
To kill Lorenzo, and there bury him.

XXIII

So on a pleasant morning, as he leant
Into the sunrise, o'er the balustrade
Of the garden-terrace, towards him they bent
Their footing through the dews; and to him said,
'You seem there in the quiet of content,
Lorenzo, and we are most loth to invade
Calm speculation; but if you are wise,
Bestride your steed while cold is in the skies.

XXIV

'To-day we purpose, ay, this hour we mount
To spur three leagues towards the Apennine;
Come down, we pray thee, ere the hot sun count
His dewy rosary on the eglantine.'
Lorenzo, courteously as he was wont,
Bowed a fair greeting to these serpents' whine;
And went in haste, to get in readiness,
With belt, and spur, and bracing huntsman's dress.

XXV

And as he to the court-yard passed along,
Each third step did he pause, and listened oft
If he could hear his lady's matin-song,
Or the light whisper of her footstep soft;
And as he thus over his passion hung,
He heard a laugh full musical aloft,
When, looking up, he saw her features bright
Smile through an in-door lattice, all delight.

XXVI

'Love, Isabel!' said he, 'I was in pain
Lest I should miss to bid thee a good morrow:
Ah! What if I should lose thee, when so fain
I am to stifle all the heavy sorrow
Of a poor three hours' absence? but we'll gain
Out of the amorous dark what day doth borrow.
Good bye! I'll soon be back.' 'Goodbye!' said she –
And as he went she chanted merrily.

XXVII

So the two brothers and their murdered man
Rode past fair Florence, to where Arno's stream
Gurgles through straitened banks, and still doth fan
Itself with dancing bulrush, and the bream
Keeps head against the freshets. Sick and wan
The brothers' faces in the ford did seem,
Lorenzo's flush with love. – They passed the water
Into a forest quiet for the slaughter.

XXVIII

There was Lorenzo slain and buried in,
There in that forest did his great love cease.
Ah! when a soul doth thus its freedom win,
It aches in loneliness — is ill at peace
As the break-covert blood-hounds of such sin.
They dipped their swords in the water, and did tease
Their horses homeward, with convulsed spur,
Each richer by his being a murderer.

XXIX

They told their sister how, with sudden speed,
Lorenzo had ta'en ship for foreign lands,
Because of some great urgency and need
In their affairs, requiring trusty hands.
Poor girl! put on thy stifling widow's weed,
And 'scape at once from Hope's accursed bands;
To-day thou wilt not see him, nor to-morrow,
And the next day will be a day of sorrow.

XXX

She weeps alone for pleasures not to be;
Sorely she wept until the night came on,
And then, instead of love, O misery!
She brooded o'er the luxury alone:
His image in the dusk she seemed to see,
And to the silence made a gentle moan,
Spreading her perfect arms upon the air,
And on her couch low murmuring 'Where? O where?'

XXXI

But Selfishness, Love's cousin, held not long
Its fiery vigil in her single breast.
She fretted for the golden hour, and hung
Upon the time with feverish unrest –
Not long – for soon into her heart a throng
Of higher occupants, a richer zest,
Came tragic – passion not to be subdued,
And sorrow for her love in travels rude.

XXXII

In the mid days of Autumn, on their eves
The breath of Winter comes from far away,
And the sick west continually bereaves
Of some gold tinge, and plays roundelay
Of death among the bushes and the leaves,
To make all bare before he dares to stray
From his north cavern. So sweet Isabel
By gradual decay from beauty fell,

XXXIII

Because Lorenzo came not. Oftentimes
She asked her brothers, with an eye all pale,
Striving to be itself, what dungeon climes
Could keep him off so long? They spake a tale
Time after time, to quiet her. Their crimes
Came on them, like a smoke from Hinnom's vale;
And every night in dreams they groaned aloud,
To see their sister in her snowy shroud.

XXXIV

And she had died in drowsy ignorance,
But for a thing more deadly dark than all.
It came like a fierce potion, drunk by chance,
Which saves a sick man from the feathered pall
For some few gasping moments; like a lance,
Waking an Indian from his cloudy hall
With cruel pierce, and bringing him again
Sense of the gnawing fire at heart and brain.

XXXV

It was a vision. – In the drowsy gloom,
The dull of midnight, at her couch's foot
Lorenzo stood, and wept: the forest tomb
Had marred his glossy hair which once could shoot
Lustre into the sun, and put cold doom
Upon his lips, and taken the soft lute
From his lorn voice, and past his loamed ears
Had made a miry channel for his tears.

XXXVI

Strange sound it was, when the pale shadow spake;
For there was striving, in its piteous tongue,
To speak as when on earth it was awake,
And Isabella on its music hung.
Languour there was in it, and tremulous shake,
As in a palsied Druid's harp unstrung;
And through it moaned a ghostly under-song,
Like hoarse night-gusts sepulchral briars among.

XXXVII

Its eyes, though wild, were still all dewy bright
With love, and kept all phantom fear aloof
From the poor girl by magic of their light,
The while it did unthread the horrid woof
Of the late darkened time – the murderous spite
Of pride and avarice, the dark pine roof
In the forest, and the sodden turfed dell,
Where, without any word, from stabs he fell.

XXXVIII

Saying moreover, 'Isabel, my sweet!
Red whortle-berries droop above my head,
And a large flint-stone weighs upon my feet;
Around me beeches and high chestnuts shed
Their leaves and prickly nuts; a sheep-fold bleat
Comes from beyond the river to my bed:
Go, shed one tear upon my heather-bloom,
And it shall comfort me within the tomb.

XXXIX

'I am a shadow now, alas! alas!
Upon the skirts of human-nature dwelling
Alone. I chant alone the holy mass
While little sounds of life are round me knelling,
And glossy bees at noon do fieldward pass,
And many a chapel bell the hour is telling,
Painting me through: those sounds grow strange to me,
And thou art distant in humanity.

XL

'I know what was, I feel full well what is,
And I should rage, if spirits could go mad;
Though I forget the taste of earthly bliss,
That paleness warms my grave, as though I had
A seraph chosen from the bright abyss
To be my spouse: thy paleness makes me glad;
Thy beauty grows upon me, and I feel
A greater love through all my essence steal.'

XLI

The Spirit mourn'd 'Adieu!' – dissolved and left
The atom darkness in a slow turmoil;
As when of healthful midnight sleep bereft,
Thinking on rugged hours and fruitless toil,
We put our eyes into a pillowy cleft,
And see the spangly gloom froth up and boil:
It made sad Isabella's eyelids ache,
And in the dawn she started up awake –

XLII

'Ha! ha!' said she, 'I knew not this hard life,
I thought the worst was simple misery;
I thought some Fate with pleasure or with strife
Portioned us – happy days, or else to die;
But there is crime – a brother's bloody knife!
Sweet Spirit, thou hast schooled my infancy:
I'll visit thee for this, and kiss thine eyes,
And greet thee morn and even in the skies.'

XLIII

When the full morning came, she had devised
How she might secret to the forest hie;
How she might find the clay, so dearly prized,
And sing to it one latest lullaby;
How her short absence might be unsurmised,
While she the inmost of the dream would try.
Resolved, she took with her an aged nurse,
And went into that dismal forest-hearse.

XLIV

See, as they creep along the river side,
How she doth whisper to that aged dame,
And, after looking round the champaign wide,
Shows her a knife. – 'What feverous hectic flame
Burns in thee, child? What good can thee betide,
That thou shouldst smile again?' The evening came,
And they had found Lorenzo's earthy bed –
The flint was there, the berries at his head.

XLV

Who hath not loitered in a green church-yard,
And let his spirit, like a demon-mole,
Work through the clayey soil and gravel hard,
To see skull, coffined bones, and funeral stole;
Pitying each form that hungry Death hath marred
And filling it once more with human soul?
Ah! this is holiday to what was felt
When Isabella by Lorenzo knelt.

XLVI

She gazed into the fresh-thrown mould, as though
One glance did fully all its secrets tell;
Clearly she saw, as other eyes would know
Pale limbs at bottom of a crystal well;
Upon the murderous spot she seemed to grow,
Like to a native lily of the dell —
Then with her knife, all sudden, she began
To dig more fervently than misers can.

XLVII

Soon she turned up a soiled glove, whereon
Her silk had played in purple phantasies,
She kissed it with a lip more chill than stone,
And put it in her bosom, where it dries
And freezes utterly unto the bone
Those dainties made to still an infant's cries:
Then 'gan she work again, nor stayed her care,
But to throw back at times her veiling hair.

XLVIII

That old nurse stood beside her wondering,
Until her heart felt pity to the core
At sight of such a dismal labouring,
And so she kneeled, with her locks all hoar,
And put her lean hands to the horrid thing.
Three hours they laboured at this travail sore —
At last they felt the kernel of the grave,
And Isabella did not stamp and rave.

XLIX

Ah! wherefore all this wormy circumstance?
Why linger at the yawning tomb so long?
O for the gentleness of old Romance,
The simple plaining of a minstrel's song!
Fair reader, at the old tale take a glance,
For here, in truth, it doth not well belong
To speak – O turn thee to the very tale,
And taste the music of that vision pale.

L

With duller steel than the Persean sword
They cut away no formless monster's head,
But one, whose gentleness did well accord
With death, as life. The ancient harps have said,
Love never dies, but lives, immortal Lord:
If Love impersonate was ever dead,
Pale Isabella kissed it, and low moaned.
'Twas Love – cold, dead indeed, but not dethroned.

LI

In anxious secrecy they took it home,
And then the prize was all for Isabel.
She calmed its wild hair with a golden comb,
And all around each eye's sepulchral cell
Pointed each fringed lash; the smeared loam
With tears, as chilly as a dripping well,
She drenched away – and still she combed, and kept
Sighing all day – and still she kissed, and wept.

LII

Then in a silken scarf – sweet with the dews
Of precious flowers plucked in Araby,
And divine liquids come with odorous ooze
Through the cold serpent-pipe refreshfully –
She wrapped it up; and for its tomb did choose
A garden-pot, wherein she laid it by,
And covered it with mould, and o'er it set
Sweet basil, which her tears kept ever wet.

LIII

And she forgot the stars, the moon, and sun,
And she forgot the blue above the trees,
And she forgot the dells where waters run,
And she forgot the chilly autumn breeze;
She had no knowledge when the day was done,
And the new morn she saw not, but in peace
Hung over her sweet basil evermore,
And moistened it with tears unto the core.

LIV

And so she ever fed it with thin tears,
Whence thick, and green, and beautiful it grew,
So that it smelt more balmy than its peers
Of basil-tufts in Florence; for it drew
Nurture besides, and life, from human fears,
From the fast mouldering head there shut from view:
So that the jewel, safely casketed,
Came forth, and in perfumed leafits spread.

LV

O Melancholy, linger here awhile!
O Music, Music, breathe despondingly!
O Echo, Echo, from some sombre isle,
Unknown, Lethean, sigh to us – O sigh!
Spirits in grief, lift up your heads, and smile.
Lift up your heads, sweet Spirits, heavily
And make a pale light in your cypress glooms,
Tinting with silver wan your marble tombs.

LVI

Moan hither, all ye syllables of woe,
From the deep throat of sad Melpomene!
Through bronzed lyre in tragic order go,
And touch the strings into a mystery;
Sound mournfully upon the winds and low;
For simple Isabel is soon to be
Among the dead. She withers, like a palm
Cut by an Indian for its juicy balm.

LVII

O leave the palm to wither by itself;
Let not quick winter chill its dying hour! –
It may not be – those Baälites of pelf,
Her brethren, noted the continual shower
From her dead eyes; and many a curious elf,
Among her kindred, wondered that such dower
Of youth and beauty should be thrown aside
By one marked out to be a Noble's bride.

LVIII

And, furthermore, her brethren wondered much
Why she sat drooping by the basil green,
And why it flourished, as by magic touch.
Greatly they wondered what the thing might mean:
They could not surely give belief, that such
A very nothing would have power to wean
Her from her own fair youth, and pleasures gay,
And even remembrance of her love's delay.

LIX

Therefore they watched a time when they might sift
This hidden whim; and long they watched in vain:
For seldom did she go to chapel-shrift,
And seldom felt she any hunger-pain;
And when she left, she hurried back, as swift
As bird on wing to breast its eggs again;
And, patient as a hen-bird, sat her there
Beside her basil, weeping through her hair.

LX

Yet they contrived to steal the basil-pot,
And to examine it in secret place.
The thing was vile with green and livid spot,
And yet they knew it was Lorenzo's face:
The guerdon of their murder they had got,
And so left Florence in a moment's space,
Never to turn again. Away they went,
With blood upon their heads, to banishment.

LXI

O Melancholy, turn thine eyes away!
O Music, Music, breathe despondingly!
O Echo, Echo, on some other day,
From isles Lethean, sigh to us – O sigh!
Spirits of grief, sing not your 'Well-a-way!'
For Isabel, sweet Isabel, will die –
Will die a death too lone and incomplete,
Now they have ta'en away her basil sweet.

LXII

Piteous she looked on dead and senseless things,
Asking for her lost basil amorously;
And with melodious chuckle in the strings
Of her lorn voice, she oftentimes would cry
After the pilgrim in his wanderings,
To ask him where her basil was, and why
'Twas hid from her: 'For cruel 'tis,' said she,
To steal my basil-pot away from me.'

LXIII

And so she pined, and so she died forlorn,
Imploring for her basil to the last.
No heart was there in Florence but did mourn
In pity of her love, so overcast.
And a sad ditty on this story born
From mouth to mouth through all the country passed:
Still is the burthen sung – 'O cruelty,
To steal my basil-pot away from me!'

On a Leander Gem which Miss Reynolds my Kind Friend, Gave Me

COME HITHER, all sweet maidens soberly,
Down-looking – ay, and with a chastened light
Hid in the fringes of your eyelids white,
And meekly let your fair hands joined be,

Are ye so gentle that ye could not see,
Untouched, a victim of your beauty bright –
Sinking away to his young spirit's night,
Sinking bewildered 'mid the dreary sea:
'Tis young Leander toiling to his death.
Nigh swooning, he doth purse his weary lips
For Hero's cheek, and smiles against her smile.
O horrid dream! see how his body dips
Dead-heavy; arms and shoulders gleam awhile:
He's gone: up bubbles all his amorous breath!

To Leigh Hunt, Esq.

GLORY AND loveliness have passed away;
For if we wander out in early morn,
No wreathed incense do we see upborne
Into the east to meet the smiling day:
No crowds of nymphs soft voiced and young, and gay,
In woven baskets bringing ears of corn,
Roses, and pinks, and violets, to adorn
The shrine of Flora in her early May.
But there are left delights as high as these,
And I shall ever bless my destiny,
That in a time when under pleasant trees
Pan is no longer sought, I feel a free,
A leafy luxury, seeing I could please
With these poor offerings, a man like thee.

The Eve of St Agnes

———— EXTRACT ————

I

ST AGNES' EVE – Ah, bitter chill it was!
The owl, for all his feathers, was a-cold;
The hare limped trembling through the frozen grass,
And silent was the flock in woolly fold:
Numb were the Beadsman's fingers while he told
His rosary, and while his frosted breath,
Like pious incense from a censer old,
Seemed taking flight for heaven without a death,
Past the sweet Virgin's picture, while his prayer he saith.

II

His prayer he saith, this patient, holy man;
Then takes his lamp, and riseth from his knees,
And back returneth, meagre, barefoot, wan,
Along the chapel aisle by slow degrees:
The sculptured dead, on each side, seem to freeze,
Emprisoned in black, purgatorial rails:
Knights, ladies, praying in dumb orat'ries,
He passeth by; and his weak spirit fails
To think how they may ache in icy hoods and mails.

VI

They told her how, upon St Agnes' Eve,
Young virgins might have visions of delight,
And soft adorings from their loves receive
Upon the honeyed middle of the night,
If ceremonies due they did aright;
As, supperless to bed they must retire,
And couch supine their beauties, lily white;
Nor look behind, nor sideways, but require
Of Heaven with upward eyes for all that they desire.

XIV

'St Agnes! Ah! it is St Agnes' Eve –
Yet men will murder upon holy days:
Thou must hold water in a witch's sieve,
And be liege-lord of all the Elves and Fays,
To venture so: it fills me with amaze
To see thee, Porphyro! – St Agnes' Eve!
God's help! my lady fair the conjuror plays
This very night. Good angels her deceive!
But let me laugh awhile, I've mickle time to grieve.'

XXVIII

Stolen to this paradise, and so entranced,
Porphyro gazed upon her empty dress,
And listened to her breathing, if it chanced
To wake into a slumbrous tenderness;
Which when he heard, that minute did he bless,
And breathed himself: then from the closet crept,
Noiseless as fear in a wide wilderness
And over the hushed carpet, silent, stepped,
And 'tween the curtains peeped, where, lo! – how fast
she slept.

XLI

They glide, like phantoms into the wide hall;
Like phantoms to the iron porch they glide;
Where lay the Porter, in uneasy sprawl,
With a huge empty flaggon by his side:
The wakeful bloodhound rose, and shook his hide,
But his sagacious eye an inmate owns.
By one, and one, the bolts full easy slide –
The chains lie silent on the foot worn stones;
The key turns, and the door upon its hinges groans.

XLII

And they are gone – ay, ages long ago
These lovers fled away into the storm.
That night the Baron dreamt of many a woe,
And all his warrior-guests, with shade and form
Of witch, and demon, and large coffin-worm,
Were long be-nightmared. Angela the old
Died palsy-twitched, with meagre face deform;
The Beadsman, after thousand aves told,
For aye unsought for slept among his ashes cold.

The Fall of Hyperion. A Dream

EXTRACT

CANTO I

FANATICS HAVE their dreams, wherewith they weave
A paradise for a sect, the savage too
From forth the loftiest fashion of his sleep
Guesses at Heaven; pity these have not
Traced upon vellum or wild Indian leaf
The shadows of melodious utterance.
But bare of laurel they live, dream, and die;
For Poesy alone can tell her dreams,
With the fine spell of words alone can save
Imagination from the sable charm
And dumb enchantment. Who alive can say,
'Thou art a Poet – mayst not tell thy dreams'?
Since every man whose soul is not a clod
Hath visions, and would speak, if he have loved,
And been well nurtured in his mother tongue.
Whether the dream now purposed to rehearse
Be Poet's or Fanatic's will be known
When this warm scribe my hand is in the grave.

La Belle Dame sans Merci.
A Ballad

O WHAT CAN ail thee, knight-at-arms,
Alone and palely loitering?
The sedge has withered from the lake,
And no birds sing.

O what can ail thee, knight-at-arms,
So haggard and so woe-begone?
The squirrel's granary is full,
And the harvest's done.

I see a lily on thy brow,
With anguish moist and fever-dew,
And on thy cheeks a fading rose
Fast witherith too.

I met a lady in the meads,
Full beautiful – a faery's child,
Her hair was long, her foot was light,
And her eyes were wild.

I made a garland for her head,
And bracelets too, and fragrant zone;
She looked at me as she did love,
And made sweet moan.

I set here on my pacing steed,
And nothing else saw all day long,
For sidelong would she bend, and sing
A faery's song.

She found me roots of relish sweet,
And honey wild, and manna-dew,
And sure in language strange she said –
'I love thee true'.

She took me to her elfin grot,
And there she wept and sighed full sore,
And there I shut her wild wild eyes
With kisses four.

And there he lulled me asleep
And there I dreamed – Ah! woe betide! –
The latest dream I ever dreamt
On the cold hill side.

I saw pale kings and princes too,
Pale warriors, death-pale were they all;
They cried – 'La Belle Dame sans Merci
Thee hath in thrall!'

I saw their starved lips in the gloam,
With horrid warning gaped wide,
And I awoke and found me here,
On the cold hill's side.

And this is why I sojourn here
Alone and palely loitering,
Though the sedge is withered from the lake,
And no birds sing.

Index of First Lines

Notes on Illustrations